we

all

need

healing

# we
# all
# need
# healing

Ebube Agu

WORDS
RHYMES &
RHYTHM

National Library of Nigeria Cataloguing-in-
Publication Data

Cover Design: Schucks Media

(ALL works herein by Ebube Agu except 'False Start
III' by Chisom Nwobodo)

Printed and Published in Nigeria by:
Words Rhymes & Rhythm Limited
Suite C309, Global Plaza Plot 366, Obafemi
Awolowo Way, Jabi District, Abuja, Nigeria.
08169027757, 08060109295
www.wrr.ng

# TABLE OF CONTENTS

# DEDICATION

To Chisom,
    *Who touched my heart...*
    *And helped me heal*


And to everyone like me, in need of healing;
May you find the Joy that numbs the pain
May you find the Faith that makes you see again
May you find the Peace that lightens the weight
And may you find the Love that expels the hate

# THANK YOU!

Abba, my Father and God, for being the KING of this project from start to finish...

My Loving parents Engr. Okeoma and Mrs. Eunice Agu, for the mind-blowing love and support you gave me in too many ways to count...

Chisom Nwobodo, for being a FRIEND in every sense of the word and for being the best muse a writer could ever ask for, and Olalekan Odutusin, for being a pillar and spurring me on all through this work...

Osione Abokhai, Uju Okafor, Toluwani Obayan, Ozioma Benson, Chisom Nwobodo for your time, counsel and insight in editing this book...

Mrs. Eunice Agu, Ven. Arc & Mrs. Godson C. Okoli, Arc. J.O. Iroro, Love Ojimba, Arc. Mrs. Onyi Diribe, Lady Comfort Ekpunobi, Mr. Kelechi and Barr. Ebere Agu (and many others) for considering this a worthy investment...

Mr. Kukogho Samson of *Word, Rhymes & Rhythm Publishers,* for the honesty and efficiency with which you carried out this project and *Schucks Media* for creating a masterpiece for a cover art...

My Family, Friends, Supporters, Readers and Everyone that has in one or the other being part of my journey these last 25 Years...

THANK YOU!

# FACING REALITY

How does one face "Reality"?
Does it exist, or only in fantasy?
Is it a person or a place?
Is there one for every phase?

Who is to say what Reality is?
Who has the answers, who has the keys?
Is reality only what can be seen?
Or is it in what we really dream?

# A WORLD THAT WAS NEVER MADE

If You EVER doubt my Love for You
>    You should also doubt the air you breathe

If You EVER question my Loyalty to You
>    You should also question the ground upon
>    which you stand

If You EVER second guess my Choice of You
>    You should also second guess your Name

If You EVER imagine a world where I'm not by your
side, forever
>    Then, also imagine a world that was never
>    made

## HANDICAPPED

I don't need eyes to see
I have my Mind for that
    I don't need legs to move
    I have my will for that
        I don't need a car to drive me
        I have my Purpose for that

I don't need hands to touch
I have my Words for that
    I don't need the world to believe
    I have my Faith for that
        I have ALL I'll ever need
        And that's that about that!

# I'VE DECIDED TO BE LOVED

It's hard to find Acceptance
It's Crazy to find Love

Some choose Acceptance
Others cling to Love

I don't know much, but even if I'm not
accepted
I've decided to be Loved

# WE ALL NEED HEALING

The past didn't matter, nor did the future count...
The moment I said *"there was no us"*
Was the same I was thrown under the bus

How could that have been Love?
How can one claim that such a feeling came from
above?

How can there be a thin line between Love and Hate?
The truth is, Love is LIGHT but the other is dead
Weight

You see what I did there, *'Love is Light'*?
That would mean without it, the darkness of hate
would be in plain sight

The only way one can thrive in darkness is to be part
of it
For the very moment you involve light what you've
done is to expel the hate

With Love there's no counterfeit, Love cannot be fake
It's simple, if it's not Love, then it's Hate for goodness
sake

Love is Humble, Forgiving, Selfless and Kind
All the things that are foreign to mankind

There's only one way to thrive in the Light of Love for
real
Give in to Love, expel the hate, and then... begin to
heal!

# I PRAY!

*(For My Family)*


I Pray Nature is Kind to you (Mother)
I Pray the rains fall on you
I Pray the winds blow your way
I Pray

I Pray Nature Favors you (Father)
I Pray the roads are clear for you
I Pray the sun shines bright for you
I Pray

I Pray Nature Rewards you (Sister)
I Pray Your kids grow Wise and Strong
I Pray your harvest is bountiful & long
I Pray

I Pray Nature Notices You (Brother)
I Pray your footsteps on the earth are blessed
I Pray your impact on the world is felt
I Pray

*(Nature Be Kind To Us...We Pray).*

# MY SPARK!

Like the preacher said
*'Many waters cannot quench this Love.'*

And all my dear heart ever desired
You embodied and became

You are the beam in the alley,
You are my Spark.

You are the smile in the darkness
You light up my life

Now and always
It would always be us

Eternity knows our story
Cause we walked in it

History speaks of us
Cause we made it

Nature bows to us
Cause we defied it

Hope belongs to us
Cause we have it

And Love allies with us
Cause we fell in it

To Beauty, Completion, Perfection
To the one who has won my affection

# I'D RATHER HOPE...

*'Don't hope for too much,'* they said
*'You will get disappointed,'* they said

> I'd rather Hope that tomorrow will be better
> than today
> I'd rather Hope that, no matter what, there'll
> always be a way
> I'd rather Hope for sun on a rainy day
> I'd rather Hope for light, I'd wait for a ray
> I'd rather Hope for Hope, come what may
> I'd rather hope and keep hoping that my hope
> will pay

# DIFFICULT PEOPLE

*Life is not difficult, people are*

It is people who say *"flabbergasted"* instead of *"surprised"*
It is people who say *"Let me think about it"* instead of a simple *"No"*
It is people that force themselves to wear what others admire
It is people that go bankrupt, borrowing to 'belong'
It is people that date with no intentions of marriage
It is people that don't study but expect great results

It is people that drive recklessly but pray for God's protection
It is people that wait for a girl's wedding day to proclaim their affection
It is people that borrow with no real plans of paying back
It is people that don't take responsibility, and that's a fact
It is people that will forgo purpose and go in search of pleasures
It is people that forsake happiness and give into life's pressures

*You see, Life is not difficult. People are!*

## SOMETHING NEW

I've decided to try something new
Before now it was never really in view
But why should the past control the future?
All I need do is shift my focus and change the old
Picture

I've decided to try something new
To start something as fresh as the morning dew
Right now I may not fully understand why
But one thing I'm sure of is that I must try!

# I WILL NOT DO IT...

*I will not do it, I will not do it*

That thing that will make you frown
*I will not do it*
That thing that will bring you down
*I will not do it*

*I will not do it, I will not do it*

Those silly things that make you mad
*I will not do it*
Those mean things that leave you sad
*I will not do it*

*I will not do it, I will not do it*

Not listen to every word you say
*I will not do it*
Forget to call you everyday
*No, I will not do it...*

# *TWINKLE TWINKLE*

Twinkle twinkle notification star
Oh I wonder what you are
Instagram, Facebook or a bae?
Have you come to take my mind away?

Twinkle twinkle notification star
You got me last time, you took me far
Not this time, No! You won't get my attention
I am applying control, I'm learning moderation

# HILLS & VALLEYS

We Meet, We Like, We Date, We Love
Then…
We Argue, Fight, Split and Dissolve

When does it end, this constant flux?
When we decide and say so of course.
When we erase thoughts like "unresolvable"
When we refuse excuses like "incompatible"

It ends when...
We Meet, We Like, We Date, We Love
Then…
We Argue, Fight, Pause and Resolve

This is the way that things should go
This is the order in which Love should flow
Love is not a bed of roses as they say
Love is a road with Hills and Valleys along its way

# I HATE THAT HEARTS GET BROKEN

I hate that hearts get broken
I hate that hurtful words get spoken
I hate that men lie and cheat and don't keep their word
I hate that women gossip and nag; I think it's just
absurd

I hate that hearts get broken, I said to her
Why can't we choose to be true to who we are?
Why can't we trash the wrong & choose the right?
Why can't we leave the dark & walk in light?

I hate that hearts get broken, I said to him
It happens when selfishness swallows love deep
within
If we all treat others like we treat ourselves
We'd love & share, & most of all care!

When less hearts get broken, and Love is revealed
Less people will be shattered and more will be healed.

# RETROSPECTION

Sometimes I wonder: what could have been?
What if I'd waited, what if I was keen?
Sometimes I wonder, what could have been
If I'd acted with Love in every scene

Sometimes I wonder; what could have been?
If I held on to that sweet dream?
Maybe if I had a clue, just maybe if I'd stayed true
Right now I won't live in a world, where there is no
You...

# I AM HOPE!

Hi, I'm *Lara*
I'm Impoverished
Discouraged &
Abandoned.

Hello, I'm *Ahmed*
I'm Molested
Frustrated &
Disoriented.

Hey! I'm *Ndidi*
I'm Sick
Orphaned &
Helpless.

Hi *Lara*
Hello Ahmed
Hey Ndidi

I'm the Future
I Am Tomorrow
I Am HOPE!

# *I AM HERE*

I did not come to tell tales
I did not come to answer a roll call
I did not come to be noticed
I did not come to get qualified.

I have come to make a lasting impact
I have come to change the system
I have come to bring healing
I have come to be of service

I am not just a member
I am not merely passing through
I am not here to manage
I am not here to pass time

I am here to lend a helping hand
I am here to be a needed voice
I am here to stand for truth in humility
I am here! And I am here for service.

*Dedicated to the National Youth Service Corps (NYSC)*

# SPECULATION

What if I told you how you make me feel?
What if I wasn't scared of what might be?
What if I didn't see you in my dreams each night?
What if I had courage to share my plight?

What if you saw me the way I saw you?
What if you were my pink, and I your blue?
What if you reached out and gave me your hand?
What if I wasn't just building castles in the sand?

What if I came and took you in my arms?
What if I wrote you a letter of all my plans?
What if all along you've waited for me?
Or what if we were just never meant to be?

What if...

## NOSY FRIENDS

I see the way your friends look at me
      I hear the way they speak of me
      They think I'm no good for you
      They think I'm not right for you

I see the way you stand up for me
      And the way you speak of me
      You tell them I'm sensational
      You tell them I'm phenomenal

Now I care less what your friends think
      I care less what they say
      Knowing what you really think
      That keeps me going each day.

# *YOUR FATHER HATES ME!*

Your Father Hates Me!
Oh, it's clear to see

Don't you see how he treats me with guile?
Like how he made us wait 7 years
        to walk down the aisle

Have you forgotten when he said
        that poverty favors me?
Or when he said my trousers were as skinny
        as my bank account would ever be?

Just the other day he ridiculed my profession
He said thinking about what I do gives him depression
But what did I ever do to make him hate me so?
Is it really because of me
        or he simply can't let (You) go?

# LINES...

The World is full of lines
*Hair lines,*
*Deadlines,*
*Life lines &*
*Pick up lines*

Hair lines are good
when they're not playing peekaboo

Deadlines aren't scary
when you've done what you should do

Life lines are awesome –
everyone wants some too

But pick-up lines are hard...
harder when they have to come from you

# SIDE DISH

Tell me the truth
Do you really Love me?

I don't think our feelings are the same
I think to you, this is all a game

I spend almost all I have buying you gifts
You spend more than half the time having a beef

Do you really Love me?
Cos you never introduce me
Tell me what I am to you
Tell me this, and please be true

Tell me the Truth
Do you really Love me?
Cos you never let us eat out, you insist we order in
You never let me take pictures, you say it's bothering

Tell me the truth
Do you really Love me?
Cos you treat me like a side dish
You make me feel like a bad wish

Whatever it is, I can't take it any more
Tell me the truth now
Or I walk out the door...
DO YOU REALLY LOVE ME?

# 17, 18, 19

*17, 18, 19*
These girls won't kill us
They move and sway
To the beats their *'koi koi'* makes

*17, 18, 19*
Where did they learn these steps?
Or were they born with it?
What makes their moves such a hit?

*17, 18, 19*
They make looking around so daunting
Do these girls walk in order to move?
Or do they aim to kill with the way they groove?

*('Koi koi'*- Nigerian slang for "Stilettos")

# STORIES I WISH TO TELL

There are stories I wish to tell...
They're stuck to my mind
Like a man behind bars
This man can see the gates,
He sees the cars come and go
He catches glimpses of hawkers
And children going to school
He hears the sound of the buses
And sometimes sees a plane
He sees their smiles
And sometimes feels their pain

There are stories I wish to tell...
They're lodged in my throat
Like a tenant who never pays
Stories of a good deal
Suddenly turned bad
Stories of a great man
And the Glory he had
Stories of a journey to a place unknown
Stories of a tale that's never been told

There are stories I wish to tell...
I hang on to them
Like a man hanging off a cliff
Every move is deliberate
Every breath delicate
This man is in no mood for games
He has no time to play
All he has is a grip
That's slowly fading away

There are stories I wish to tell…
Stories of a woman, a woman barren
For 58 years & counting, she's never stopped trying
These are no random tales, they're not tales of woe
They're stories of a nation let FREE to grow
Stories of a people held down by YESTERDAY
Stories of choices yet to be made TODAY
Stories of my country, stories of TOMORROW
Stories that I hope will not end in Sorrow

Nigeria is a story I wish to tell...

# WE ARE THE ONES

We are the ones who've been let down
    We are the ones who've been betrayed
        We are the ones who've been heartbroken
            We are the ones who've been misled

We are the ones who were lied to
    We are the ones who were left out
        We are the ones who were less privileged
            We are the ones who were written off

We are the ones still standing
    We are the ones still dreaming
        We are the ones still moving
            We are the ones still here

*We are the ones...*

# TANTRUMS

She was bent on throwing tantrums
Pity I didn't care enough to catch them
She always found one to throw
And hoped I would join the game

I made that mistake once
To walk down that road
Now when she throws her tantrums
I just hit it home with Love

## EVERY MOTHER...

Every mother is "*the best in the world*"
We hear it all the time, it's even sung in rhymes

Best, not because she has superpowers
Best, not because she's prettier than flowers

Best, not because she provides so much money
Best, not because her meals taste better than honey

Every mother is *"the best in the world"*
Is a statement of fact, for all with Loving mothers

There's no denying it, we know it to be so
Every mother, truly, is *"the best in the world"*

# CONFESSION...

I confess that I truly did Love you
I confess that I'm still getting over you
I confess that I really wanted us to be
I confess that I loved it when you called me *"B"*

I confess that I tried to be true to you all the way
I confess that I never meant to hurt you in any way
I confess that my time with you was a blessing
I confess that I still think you're a good person

I confess that I'll always wish you well
I pray for you, and honestly hope you do well
I confess that you will always be in my heart
But now it belongs to another who won't tear it apart.

# WORDS ARE SEEDS

Words are (like) seeds
Seeds sown by a Farmer
Words are (like) deeds
Deeds that bow to Karma

What you sow is what you reap
He that sows sorrow will soon surely weep
Expecting to reap what was not sown, is the way of a
fool
But if you sow words of Joy, then your joy will be full

Words are (like) seeds
They can yield much fruit
So watch the seeds that you sow
Cos by God, they will surely grow

# YOU ONLY LIVE ONCE!

Refuse to walk this earth
without leaving a mark
Refuse to leave this world
without leaving a bang

Refuse to go round and round
without reaching the line
Refuse to be busy, but only
waste time

Refuse to Love without a
reason
Refuse to do only what is
pleasing

Refuse to cower at your
challenges
But choose to rise up and
overcome it

Refuse to allow problems
overwhelm you
Rather, choose to enjoy life as
do only a few

# VITAL LESSON

*"LEARN TO BE YOURSELF*
*It's a COURSE you must take"*

Learn that you can never portray a
better image
Than the one you already have

Learn to accept your shortcomings and
weaknesses
Learn to leverage on your strengths &
harness it

Learn to see the opportunities in front
of you
Begin to walk your path and maintain
your view

Learn that you will always fail until
you find who you are
Until you learn to be you, you will
never be above par

*"LEARN TO BE YOURSELF*

# AS WE THOUGHT...

As we thought in our hearts, so we are becoming
*"It's possible, it's Possible"* was all our hearts were
humming

We thought we could break the records set before us
We thought *"If we make History, that'll be a plus"*

We thought we could truly make global impact
So we strived to keep our attitude very intact

Look! We're doing it! Yes! We're blossoming
As we thought in our hearts, so we are becoming.

# GUTS

The sun owes me no Favors
    The moon has no debt to pay
        The winds seek not my permission
            The rains ask not for my suggestion

        The heavens lived before I did
      The earth bears me no allegiance
    The seas aren't bound to me
The fires know not my name

Yet it's a wonder all these work together
    Just to favor me
        And someone, somewhere will have the guts
        to say
            There isn't a God up there, watching over
            me

## DELIVERER

Many times I'm stuck
Stuck in a web of woes
Many times I'm locked
Locked in a dungeon of sorrows

Time and time again I fall
With nowhere to go, backed against the wall
I remember He listens, keenly awaiting my call
*"Deliverer, Deliverer, see me through it all."*

## PEPPER THEM

These girls aim to slay!
They say, *"We're going to pepper them*
*Show them who runs the world..."*

They are everywhere on the gram
So quick are they to snap & chat
Yeah, that's the life they're all about

       Fast forward! The time is 20 years later
       I see them in churches praying
       Holding pillars & shaking heads

       Asking the *"God of a second chance"*
       For another chance to slay
       And this time, slay where it counts.

...And if you fail
Get up and TRY again

...And when you crash
Get up and FLY again
       Until FAILURE gives up on you
       And SUCCESS knows your name.

Try...

# UTOPIA

I thought I Loved You
*I really did*
I thought I Loved to Love You
*I mean this*

...Until I found another who I
loved just as much

> And realized it wasn't
> really you I loved...
> I just love the idea of Love

# WHEN FAILURE KNOCKS

And when Failure knocks again
Shut your ears so tight
Shut your eyes so tight
And keep your gates shut tight

When failure knocks again
Don't answer the call
For although failure is a lesson
The ability to see it from afar
Is a much bigger blessing
I think...

## DESTINY

And when the road seems rough
When the journey seems tough
Don't stop then
It's not time for *'Amen'*
For, just a few miles ahead
Is the lady you dreamt of

She's the place called Destiny
And she's worth fighting for.

## THE LEADER

They could never understand
Why I loved you so
I could never understand
Why you never let go

*Sometimes Love isn't poetic*
*Sometimes it lacks rhythm*
*But what makes (our) Love work*
*Is that our hearts do the leading*

So, put logic far away
Abandon clear thought & reasoning
For in the course of learning to Love
The head is often misleading

## MISTAKES

I've made mistakes
        Mistakes that seemed to make me
                Make me into what I was not
                        I was not timid, I was never shy
                I was never shy, nor afraid to try
        To try out my new ideas
New ideas and Dreams
        Dreams that were so real
                So real others saw
                        Others saw My Plight
                My Plight as I sought to Succeed
        To Succeed, I've made mistakes
Mistakes… They seem to make me

# REDEEMING THE TIME

You wish you had more time
You wish time was on your side

But you fail to reckon,
That time chooses no sides

Time has no owner
It bows to no one

Time only listens
When you let Wisdom speak

# FOOL FOR LOVE

*"I don't believe in Love"*
*"I don't believe in Love"*

You think it wise that you don't believe in Love
Yet I know a fool who doesn't believe in God

The fool says there is no God
You say there is no Love

Now we know that God is Love
So where does that leave you?

# MOOD SWINGS

He screams & shouts and then he's calm
As complex as the waves of the sea
As uncertain as a ship that's lost its sails
From Left to Right his mood swings

From Left to Right her mood swings
This moment she cries & next she sings
As unstable as a plane with broken wings
From left to right her mood swings

# WHEN WORDS MEANT MUCH

When Words Meant Much
Men stuck around for their families
And fathers were not endangered

When Words Meant Much
People strived to redeem their pledges
And lies did not come cheap

When Words Meant Much
People rarely "call to cancel"
And rain checks were less

When Words Meant Much
Children did not dupe their parents
And leaders were bound to their promises

When Words Meant Much
Friendship stood for something
And loyalty was a prized possession

When Words Meant Much
Faithful men were all around
And virtuous women did abound.

When Words Meant Much…

## *SHOTS FIRED!*

Shots Fired
Words Said
Many wounded
Men Bled

If only we could point our guns in the right direction
If only we could speak with much discretion

Then we'll have less wounded & less broken
We'll have less souls that bleed from words spoken.

# NOTE TO FAILURE

...And when you come looking for me
Don't look in the slums
And don't search the valleys
Don't bother going through the dark & lonely alleys

When you come looking for me
Keep your head up, & your gaze above
I'm up like the star, I'm far from pale
No more in the shadows, now I'm blazing the trail.

## BRACE FOR IMPACT!

I wish we were labeled at birth
I wish we were prepared for this
I wish someone had said these words;
*"Brace for Impact!"*

In the course of life, you will hit rocks
In your adventures, you might get knocked
Things might not work as you wished
The World might seem to gang up on you

As you progress in the journey of Life,
Expect to meet challenges, get ready for strife
Anticipate hard times so you remain intact
And no matter happens, you better brace for Impact!

# MONSTER

Man vexed
Eyes Red
Tempers Flared
Punches Shared

Woman Weeps
Body beaten
Face Swollen
Heart broken

Boy sits
Sits & Learns
Learns the ways
The ways of 'Monster'...

Boy grows up
Becomes Man
Man vexed
'Monster' appears…

# LET THEM KNOW...

The people are crying
The masses are dying
There is panic everywhere
There is chaos in the air

The leaders are dining
See their children wining
Their houses get bigger
And their accounts fatter

There are widows on the streets
There are fathers in the slums
Their meals get smaller
And their children thinner

Can anyone find Love?
Where does Justice work?
Does anyone know Equity?
Where does Unity live?

If you get a hold of them
If you see them drive by
If you find their dwelling place
Please let them know

The people are crying
The masses are dying
There is panic everywhere
There is chaos in the air.

## BLURRED LINES

I thought you said you loved me
I thought you said you cared
I thought a promising future
Was one that we both shared

I thought you knew I liked you
As a friend and nothing more
This child you now speak of
Was not what I asked for

We thought we could play with fire
And fire would not burn us
Now fire has played with our hearts
And has left us broken, shattered & torn apart

# COUNTING THOUGHTS

Is it the thought that counts?

What if I thought of taking you to the movies every
week?
What if I said I Loved You but it's another I seek?
What if I thought of helping out with the dishes all the
time?
But instead all I do is sit and eat and write my rhymes?

Is it the thought that counts?

Will schools ever reward students who only think of
studying?
Will banks ever pay the penniless that are always
bothering?
Would merchants ever take payments made in
shiploads of thought?
Or would they arrest the buyer until they pay for all
they bought?

Is it just the thought that's really going to count?
Or the effort in birthing what one thought about?
Is it just okay for great thoughts to abound?
Or isn't it the actions that make the thoughts to count?

# UNBREAKABLE

I grew up in a home, a home filled with Love
It was full of warmth, laughter and peace from above
This home was laden with problems that threatened to
make it fail

It wasn't perfect in every way; it was not a fairy tale
Voices were raised and toes stepped upon
But forgiveness always spoke up, no matter what was
done

This is that home, the one filled with Love
The one with warmth, laughter and peace from above
The storms attacked, but Love thrived
Offenses came, yet Love survived

Now I see Love not as a movie
I see it not as a piece of art
I see Love as a home
Which can never be torn apart

# RAT RACE

Sometimes it's not the bad
That makes you sad
Sometimes it's the good
That makes you brood
Because instead of seeing
The bad in you becoming good
You're focused on the good of others
Making yours look bad

*How sad...*

# SWEET PAIN...

Crying does not mean
you've lost hope

Sometimes you need to
let out the pain
Because pain was
never meant to kill you
Rather it was designed
to heal you

The healing that we
often seek
To find deep down in
the place of pleasure
Is the healing that is
sometimes buried
Deep down in pain
without measure

## *TRUE LOVE SCARES YOU*

True Love scares you
Too much love makes you afraid

That is why you rejected the one
That tried to be there for you
You pushed away the one
Who swore to die for you
But rather choose the one
Who was no good for you

True Love scares you.

# LEAP OF FAITH

You can't live life
Afraid of *"What ifs"*

They are not for you to cower
They were not meant to cripple you
They were meant to give you power
To whatever your mind can brew
They are not your enemies
They are projections of hope
They are ladders to success
They are portals to greatness

You can't live life
Afraid of *"What ifs"*

# PARASITE

You hold on to bitterness
Because you think it strengthens you
You cling to un-forgiveness
Because you think it empowers you
But the very things you rely on
These "dear" things that you harbor
They are the things that kill you
They are the things that seek to drain you

# I DO NOT BLAME YOU

I do not blame you...

It's my heart I blame
For beating tirelessly for you
My Head, for thinking relentlessly of you
And myself for falling helplessly in Love with you

# WET CONCRETE

Mind what you say
Just as you mind where you go
The mind is like wet concrete
And your words like big feet
Your steps will leave a lasting mark
For all to come and see

As a builder must take care
Of the materials used in building
You must beware
Of the words you're prone to speaking

# MORE THAN WORDS

I like you
More than a child likes play

I want you
More than a lion wants prey

I love you
More than a priest loves to pray

And I need you
More than my words can say

# UNBREAK MY HEART

Unbreak my heart
Go back in time
Take a trip to Genesis
Take back those sweet words you said
Take back these thoughts in my head

Unbreak my heart
Give me back all my trust
Erase the day our paths crossed
Wipe me off your mind too
And make me forget I Love You

# UNDENIABLE

If Samson was a weakling
And Solomon a fool

If David was a coward
And Hell Fire was cool

Only then can it be said
That I don't Love You

# *FANTASY*

I believe in dreams
And I believe in Fantasies
I believe a woman can be left
To define who she should be
I believe a man has the right
To imagine all he can be

I believe in dreams
And I believe in fantasies
But after all has been said
And nothing is done
Then our dreams become nightmares
And our fantasies forgone

# EMANCIPATOR

I believe a story
Of a legend told to us
The legend of the Son
Who died on the cross
Love brought him down
But hate hung him up
High on that tree
On the tree where He was
That was where I was born
That was where my life began

I believe a story
Of a legend told to us
A Son brighter than the Sun
Who came to restore
Born of a woman
Yet God in Himself
A mystery beyond men
A miracle on earth
His life He gave for me
Now all I am is Free!

# LOVE LIVES HERE!

Love Lives Here!
Here in my crooked heart
Right here in my scattered head

Love Lives here in my *"face me"* house
Right here in my *"Legedeze Benz"*

Love Lives here in my shaky voice
Right here in my hopeful eyes

Love Lives here where you'd least expect
Right here from whom you'd soon reject

Love Lives Here!

*Face Me House- One bedroom apartments usually for low
income earners*

*Legedeze Benz- Nigerian, funny way of referring to the Legs
as being one's car)*

# THE RISE & FALL

When He first met her
He didn't fall in love with her wits
He wasn't pulled in by her vision
He wasn't wooed by her spirit

    When He first met her
    It was her pretty face he saw
    The gorgeous body she had
    Was what left him in awe

        When he first met her
        He thought she'd never grow old
        Now things are *"going down"*
        His Love also grows cold.

## I (HER)

I gave too much of me to you
I think I made it too easy
I made myself too open to you
I think I spoilt you crazy

I let myself be wooed too soon
I let my heart be nice to you
I let your words caress my mind
I let you in, when you'd barely knocked

## II (HIM)

I think I came on too strong
I think I did it all wrong
Maybe if I threaded softly
I would not have lost myself

I let myself be free with you
I let myself be entirely true
I let my wounds be shown to you
I let you in, like you did me too

## III (THEM)

We flew when we should have walked
And our feeble wings went sore
From fighting a wind we weren't trained for

We sang when we should have talked
And our tender throats went sore
From reaching a pitch we hadn't trained for

We crashed and it hurt
We fell to the ground and it burned
But we realize that's where we should be
Counting One first, then two and three

# THE STUFF OF LEGENDS

We grew up with each other
We came up the ranks together
I watched Him take shape
I listened as experience beat a boy into a man

I observed as life showed a man its secrets
I stood as Wisdom took this man by hand
Discipline snatched his life away
Hope never let him sway

Vision kidnapped him
Purity took over his home
Diligence tied him sternly
Honesty hijacked him, plainly

Now remember I said I grew up with this man
Remember we came up the ranks together
As we grew, he became a sample of what I admired
He walked paths where I only dreamed of

I literally witnessed the making of greatness
This man, is the very stuff of Legends
He is the story that will be told to generations unborn
He is the template that will be passed on to Kings to
come

He is You, He is Me, He is what every man should
strive to Be.
He is... The Stuff of Legends

# DO YOU HEAR ME?

*(For My Brother)*

Do not consider holding back
Do you hear me?
Do not contemplate growing slack

Do not cower at the raging storms
Do not sleep when danger comes
Stand and ride upon your scary seas
Stay and take honey from those nagging bees

Put it all in, you've got what it takes
Work, work, work, till your day breaks!
But NEVER consider holding back
NEVER contemplate growing slack

Do you hear me?

## BURDEN SHARER

When you claim to Love me
And ask me to Love You
Please understand what you are saying

> That I should Love, care and be there for you
> But also that I should share my burdens with
> you

Please understand what you are saying
When you claim to Love me

# IN THE EYES OF THE BEHOLDER

How real is the beauty lodged
'In the eyes of the beholder'?

What happens when the beholder is gone?
Does the beheld remain beautiful?
Or go looking for another beholder
To make her beautiful once again?
Does the beholder have power to create?
Or possess the ability to destroy?
What then happens to the beheld
When the beauty in the eyes of the beholder
Seems lost and void of all wonder?

How real is the beauty
'In the eyes of the beholder'?

# LET'S BREAK NIGHT

Let's break night my Love
Let's stay out and stare at the stars above
Let's lock hands and let our hearts beat
Let's keep shut and let our minds wander
Come on, let's break night
Let's stand forever by each other
Let's put up a fight
Stare at the firmament
As we long for daylight
Let's break night Darling,
Come on, let's break night
Let's watch as the darkness takes flight
Let's stand together as the storms dissolve
Let's break night my Love

# *WITHOUT YOU*

The Grass without Green
The Bee without Sting
The Sky without Blue
Is what I am without You.

## DOUBLE MINDED

I.

Maybe You are the road I was meant to travel
Maybe You were the gift I was meant to unravel
Maybe You are the lips I was meant to kiss
Or maybe You are the call that I should have missed

Maybe...

II.

Maybe...

Maybe You were the story I was meant to tell
Maybe You were the dream I was meant to dream
Maybe You were the song I was meant to sing
Or, Maybe You were the lesson I was meant to learn.

# *LET'S BE HONEST*

Let's be honest, Love doesn't hurt
Why would the one thing meant to be perfect give you
a cut?
Some say they hate Love, that it broke their heart
Some others say Love isn't real, that it's a work of art

Love doesn't hurt, it never did
Lies, deceit and Selfishness have choked it
Most times when people think of what Love is
It's the pain they feel that comes to mind, and not the
bliss

# GOOD OL' DAYS

*Good Ol' days, Good Ol' days*
Why do people even call you good?
Why do they think of you with such fondness?
What is it about you that brings gladness?

*Good Ol' days, Good Ol' days*
Remember when those same people lived in you?
Remember how they preferred your older ones?
Remember how they never Loved You for once?

*Good Ol' days, Good Ol' days*
I've seen that the battle is between the old and the new
It's not because of you that the people Love you
It's cos you're now old they so adore You.

It's because of the dreams they buried in you
It's because of the hopes they had in you
It's because they'd rather not work but live in Fantasy
It's because as far as dreams go, you're all they can see

# MARRY ME!

Baby Marry me

Before you say yes,
Please consider my proposal
I'm not merely asking you to say *"I do"*
It's not about fixing a date or calling me *"Boo"*

Baby Marry ME
Don't marry a fantasy
Marry the person that I am
Not just the person I could be

I am not perfect
I am not all knowing
I will not always know when something is wrong
I will not always be able to sing you a song

I may not always give the best foot rubs
In fact I may desire some of my own
I promise though, to do everything I can to make you
happy
I'll try to provide anything you'll need, I'll make it
snappy

Please don't marry my money
I cannot vouch for it
And don't marry my body
It will not always be fit

These six packs may not last till sixty
These strong arms may grow weak and weary
But my heart will always be strong and steady

Filled with nothing but Love for you my Baby

Marry my Plans, Vision and Purpose
Marry my Imperfections, Frailties and Faults
Marry this man that will always be true
Marry me baby, and I'll Always Love You

# YES! BE STUPID!

Speak before you think
*Yes! Be stupid*

Keep shooting words like arrows
*Go! Be Cupid*

Don't consider what you just heard
Don't even choose your words, no that's weird

Go on, speak before you think.
*Yes! Be stupid!*

## FORGETFUL HEART

Is it weird that I don't miss you?
Is it strange that you don't make me cry?
When you said it was all over
I really thought my life would start over

Now I try so hard to remember you
I try so hard to reminisce
But all you left behind was darkness
So, is it weird that I don't miss you?

## IF THE SUN GOES DARK

The night draws nigh, as the daylight blurs
The time flies by, as it always does

Yet
If the rains cease & the Sun goes dark
If the Mountains crumble & the Stars lose spark

My Prayers for You will never cease
My Fire for You will never quench
My Love for You will never dwindle
And my Life with You will never die.

www.ingramcontent.com/pod-product-compliance
Lightning Source LLC
Chambersburg PA
CBHW032007060426
42449CB00032B/1031